THE MADEC FAMILY LEGACY: LESSONS IN LEADERSHIP

Thomas A. Maier, PhD

AuthorHouse™
1663 Liberty Drive
Bloomington, IN 47403
www.authorhouse.com
Phone: 833-262-8899

Because of the dynamic nature of the Internet, any web addresses or links contained in
this book may have changed since publication and may no longer be valid. The views
expressed in this work are solely those of the author and do not necessarily reflect the views
of the publisher, and the publisher hereby disclaims any responsibility for them.

Any people depicted in stock imagery provided by Getty Images are models,
and such images are being used for illustrative purposes only.
Certain stock imagery © Getty Images.

This book is printed on acid-free paper.

ISBN: 978-1-6655-0651-9 (sc)
ISBN: 978-1-6655-0653-3 (hc)
ISBN: 978-1-6655-0652-6 (e)

Library of Congress Control Number: 2020921815

Print information available on the last page.

Published by AuthorHouse 12/22/2020

authorHOUSE®

The Madec Family Legacy:

Lessons in Leadership

by Thomas A. Maier PhD.

Introduction

Ostréiculteur
depuis *1898*

    This generational leadership story illuminates the amazing career of Yvon Madec and his family's historical legacy in oyster farming. Madec has forged his career while simultaneously mentoring his daughter, Caroline, who works side by side with her father at their Brittany, France oyster farm. In this book, Yvon and Caroline's leadership styles are viewed through the lens of contemporary leadership philosophy, family succession planning and enterprise management.

    Their story offers food enthusiasts and leadership professionals a unique tutorial on family centered leadership and succession planning. The book examines family business legacy and multigenerational leadership through the trials and tribulations of a world renowned *ostreiculture* [1] entrepreneur. In this multi-generational profile, Yvon Madec and his family legacy is uncovered through discovery of their unique regional terroir, the ocean and aber products they yield, and the unmatched reverence the family have toward their oysters.

    We will look deep into Yvon's craft as an oysterman and the leadership composition of father and daughter, divided by generations, yet unified by a common interest in refinement and perfection.

---

[1] French term for breeding of oysters.

Table of Contents

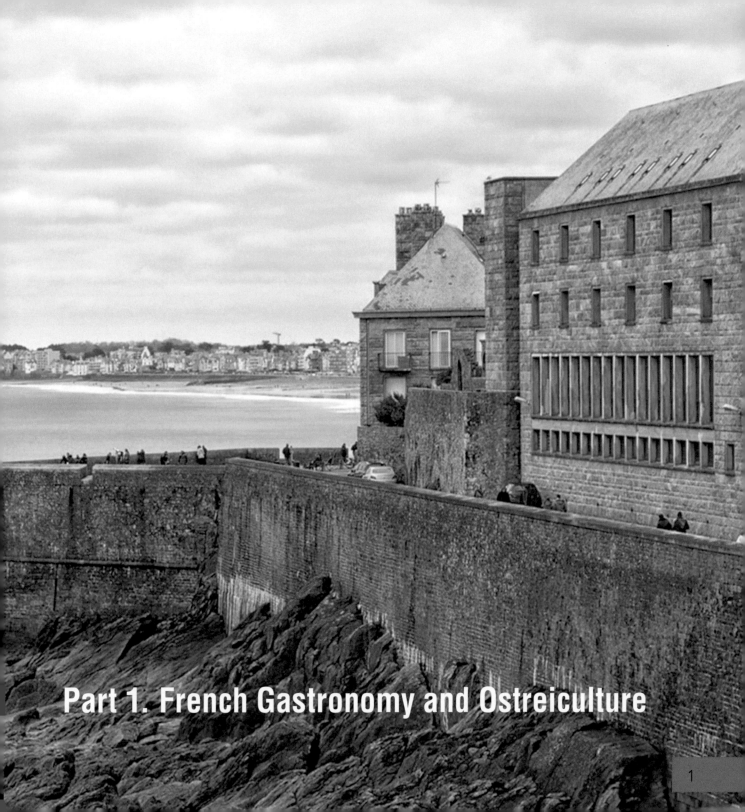

Part 1. French Gastronomy and Ostreiculture

Brittany heritage

According to renowned French geography professor Jean-Robert Pitte, "unique to France are micro-climates that are very diversified; integrating the Alpine, Mediterranean, and Atlantic agricultural components."[2] Pitte asserts that geography, among other factors, plays a significant role in enhancing the formation of gastronomy excellence, and particularly the cultural heritage of French gastronomy.

Brittany, as a province, may best be described as an area with few large towns, but rather more seaports and small villages. In Brittany, the town of Brest is a picturesque countryside village with wildflowers in bloom, thatched roof seaside cottages, small winding roads and medieval landmarks. Most of all, one is struck by the beauty of the ocean, the large sailboats and the many granite islands that belong to those fortunate enough to call Brittany home. Bretons gleefully spend holidays along the coast, and inland along the abers, relaxing at the beach and fishing. The bounty of the sea produces crab, shrimps, cockles, lobster and clams.

"In Brittany the sky is blue, in late autumn the air is sharp
and cold and when the sun begins to light the world, vision
opens all around on the high plateau one can see timothy grass
encased in small intricate robes of frost. Above and to the west
the sky is still largely obscured, but light seeps over the high plain
on which we walk and when the sun finally breaks the horizon,
the moments that follow are breathtaking." [3]

Located in the Brittany region, Prat-AR-Coum sits alongside the river of Aber-Benoît. The seagulls feast slowly and surely all day picking up shells, flying high in the sky and dropping the

---

[2] Jean-Robert Pitte, *French Gastronomy—A Hhistory and Geography of a Passion.* p.10.
[3] Ogrizek, 1948. France: Paris and the Provinces. McGraw Hill / Whittlesey House; 1st American edition

oysters to crack them open. Baby rabbits meander around the gardens by the sea, serenaded by the native birds chirping with delight.

We often hear about the importance of location in oyster farming enterprises. Situated on the edge of Brittany, Prat-AR-Coum is located in the city of Lannilis. In terms of location, the Madec family oyster farm is located on the banks of the Aber-Benoît. Abers are branches of sea which penetrate into the lands and allow the confluence of the ocean and fresh river water. The permanent exchange produced by the tides generates an abundant amount of plankton which serve as sustenance for the oysters, giving them their unique flavor. The Prat-AR-Coum oysters' fresh mix of sweetness and iodized sharpness together with its well-known taste of hazelnut, make them some of the finest oysters produced today. [4]

The historical gastronomy of Brittany celebrates the sea, whether it be the small fishing harbors, deep sea catches, or majestic abers. The culinary scene in Brittany reflects world class seafood and is also well known for crêpes. Whether sweet or savory, the infamous Brittany crêpes are made with buckwheat, or classic wheat, mostly enjoyed with salted butter-caramel, chocolate, jam or lemon. It's not uncommon to dine beachside along the rugged Brittany coast enjoying "gavottes", also called laced crêpes. These slightly overcooked crêpes, crisped to perfection, are made in the purest tradition with wheat flour, sugar and butter, paired with coffee or used to make desserts.

The Madec family business

To celebrate leadership excellence in French oyster farming, the story begins with family patriarch Yvon Madec, current oysterman at the helm of the company enterprise and the four generations before him. Understanding Yvon as a contemporary leader requires a look back in time to put his remarkable accomplishments into historical context. Much like those before him, Yvon was careful to continue the rich French tradition of oyster farming established in Prat- AR-Coum.

The Madec family business began in 1898 with Yvon's great grandfather Alain. Alain Madec challenged oyster farming notions with his neighbor M. Delamare de Bouteville, a man who most notably, was also known as the first inventor of the car motor, which he

---

[4] Ogrizek, 1948. France: Paris and the Provinces. McGraw Hill / Whittlesey House; 1st American edition

proudly displayed during the 1900 world exhibition. Yvon's father, Alain, was sixteen years old when he started working the family oyster business after his father's early death. At that time, he grew the oysters in the abers (rivers) exclusively. In 1973, Yvon Madec began learning ostréiculture beside his father. In 1985, he took the helm of Prat-AR-Coum's reins. He pursued the development of the "family enterprise" with a strong stake in the European standards and traditions that had begun generations before him. Every generation of the Madec family brought its stone to Prat-AR-Coum's building, passing on through the years the know-how of their forefathers. Henceforth, the fifth generation of the Madec family makes its entrance to the company, with Yvon's daughter Caroline.

Perhaps the most significant example of Madec's family resilience, according to Yvon was in 1970, "illness came all over the coast of Brittany forcing us to change the type of oysters from Belons to Gigas. We knew at the time that we could never give up on the Belons (Brittany's famous flat oysters), our DNA. The combination of disease and the Amoco oil disaster was very hard on the family legacy and oyster farm." Yvon recounts that perhaps the toughest time in the history of their family enterprise was the Amoco oil spill disaster, which occurred only eight miles from their land and spilled 230,000 tons of oil. As Yvon explains, "the biggest problem during the oil spill of 1978 was they had no money to fight the problem!." Many problems in their oyster "family society" occurred as a result of the Amoco oil spill. At that time, 500 tons of oysters were destroyed. As a result of the oil spill, the Madec family had no oysters in the abers until 1985. Two generations of oysters were lost. Eventually the oil spill cleanup was successful, and an unintended positive development from the spill emerged.

The Madec family diversified into the seafood trade (mussels, clams, lobster, and crab) to help bolster unpredictability and strengthen their business model. For Yvon, building the oyster farming enterprise involved more than just the multiple aqua based planting fields. The Madec family enterprise incorporates a fleet of aqua marine and heavy machinery capable of catching, barging, harvesting, sorting and planting tons of oysters per year. Yvon's favorite is his battle worn Boston whaler (water taxi) used daily to check the oyster beds and fields, shuttling between the ragged-edged Brittany coast and the tranquil abers throughout the region. The family's land-based operations include a sorting, packaging and retail store designed to serve local Bretons their favorite sampling of the freshest oysters and other bounty of the sea.

Oyster and wine pairing

Each of us shares our own taste and preference for wine and wine paired with food. There is no right or wrong selection of wine with food either. However, those specially trained in viticulture, sommeliers in particular, can recognize and detect subtle flavors and distinctions among a large variety of wines that may be unnoticed by the novice. Regardless, to know wine is to experiment and drink wine, preferably with others. France has a unique tradition of wine and wine growing. This tradition that goes hand in hand with food and wine paired together.

Kushi Oyster Concassée, Lemon and Seaweed Granité
*

Domaine Laroche Saint Martin, Chablis 2016.

Clear Iced Poached Oysters (Prat-AR-Coum)
prepared oysters set over an oyster puree and served with
seawater jelly
*

Jean Max Roger Les Caillottes, Sancerrre 2015

Steamed Belon Flats with Avocado, Horseradish and Eel
*

Domaine de Belambree Les Ephemeres Rose 2017

Freshly Harvested Aber Benoit Oysters Drizzled with
Clamato, Bacon, Horseradish & Nasturtium
*

Cave de Ribeauville Collection Riesling 2015

Part 2. Oyster Farming Fundamentals

Oysters of Prat-AR-Coum

Prat-AR-Coum oysters are unique due to their naturalness, growing time, seasonal freshness, good shape and lengthiness. The process of oyster farming is interesting, complex and fragile. Yvon explains that the oyster fields are out in the sea and the oyster beds are in the river. The foodstuffs that the oysters feed and grow on are different inside the river than in the ocean. For Yvon, the best oyster product comes from the sea, possess oceanic flavor and comes back in the abers (river) to take in the taste of the earth.

Exhibit 1. The oyster life cycle

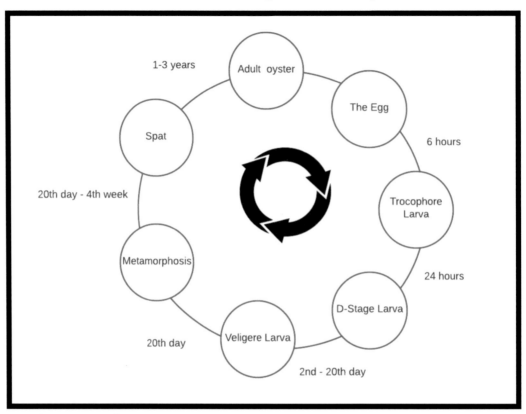

Source: https://www.francenaissain.com/en/our-production-facilities/the-r-and-d-department/

Oysters are first born in Brest, arrive to the ocean as babies and then spend one year in the ocean until they are 18 months old. The oysters subsequently go directly into the ground for one year in sacks. When the oysters are two years old, one component of the oyster returns to the river for fat ones to be constructed, and the other component stays in place to make medium-grade and large-grade oysters.

The Madec family makes both styles of oysters, Belon Ostrea Edulis and Crassostrea Gigas. They grade them and finish them in the river for that special taste of Prat-AR-Coum. According to Yvon, "what makes Prat-AR-Coum so unique is the contrast between the wild ocean and the soft river." Their oysters are unique because of their: (1) naturalness, (2) growing time, (3) seasonal freshness, and (4) good shape and lengthiness. Madec says "the craft of oyster farming is highly fragile and sensitive. In France, people enjoy the very fat oysters (*spéciales*) while some like thinner oysters (*les fines*)." This way, the Madec family is able to market two different products for customer preferences.

Oyster farming craftsmanship

Yvon embodies the generations-old Madec oyster growing philosophy "we pay careful attention to the depth and thoughtfulness in describing this relationship with the product and the history and journey of the product. As a producer we embark upon to get it to us; and what we do with it once it arrives."

Yvon, a traditional leader, is not a verbose man. If you ask and inquire, he will respond, otherwise - one must initiate the interaction with him. He has many vulnerabilities to worry about: weather, disease, regulation and tariffs. He is strong of mind and body and champion of the next generation of business. According to Yvon, the oyster farming business is very hard and unpredictable. It requires patience, stamina and resilience. He proclaims, "the craft of oyster farming is highly fragile and sensitive. Oysters are like milk on fire, we invest everything we have into the product and then entrust the chef to present them to the customer." Yvon believes ostréiculture success can be attained by keeping your feet on the ground - close to reality. Yvon values being on the job and the power of hard work, a leadership trait engrained in him by his father. These values are a true and distinguishable trait of baby boomers. Yvon knows all of the jobs required to run his family oyster business. He works the longest hours and comes in at the end of the day when all of the tasks are done, not a moment sooner. He is often the first out in the fields at sunrise and the last one out at sunset — a work ethic untouchable, but consistent among his generation.

For Yvon, the heart of his field work is the forever changing tides. The tides move gently in rhythm with the earth, offering brief glimpses of what lies beneath. Beneath the water are the expansive Madec family oyster fields, which are the lifeline of the family business. He guards those oysters as if each and every one was his precious child. The tides run in and out every 6 hours. Yvon, the oysterman, checks his tidal app - living by the sea rhythms to protect and nurture his baby oysters. He patiently awaits and carefully attends to the oysters for three years. He has hope, as he carefully handles and adapts to nature's unpredictability. A key strategy for Yvon is never putting all his oysters in one place. He divides the risk across multiple locations.

Exhibit 2. The Brittany tidal chart

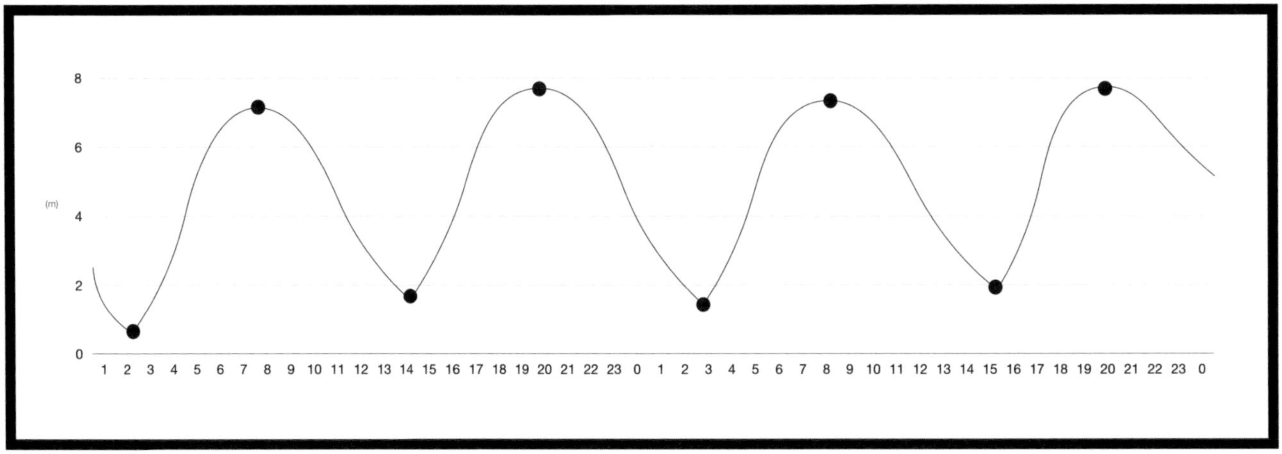

Source: https://www.tideschart.com/tides/en/Roscoff-France-tides-chart-m.png?date=20200331

Oysters, shellfish and crustaceans as a business enterprise

Oyster fields are seen near and far – the great expanse of the Madec oyster farm in Brest, Carantec, Prat-AR-Coum and the Aber Wrach. Birds are chirping and the water is quiet. Tiny little fishing boats dote the watershed landscape. Rolling green hills of hay and barley are set against the backdrop of the Breton style cottages. Picturesque and quaint, the Brittany coastal scene offers an untouched charm, with Madec's own sleepy dog on the patio. On Sunday mornings, bright and early, grandson Pol is at the Madec seafood store, weighing the oysters, shells and Dungeness crab. Family matriarch, Annie, is at the cash register while Yvon, the oysterman, is side by side with his family, talking with fellow Bretons about all the seafood they have in the shop. A seafood lover's paradise, tanks of fresh seafood, clams, oysters of various sizes, giant lobster from the Brittany channel are all a part of a day's work for the Madec family. While Yvon tends to the fields and intermittent Breton customers at the family store on weekends, the oyster business requires 24/7 attention. As like any other global business the product is one of the most important elements of a successful enterprise. Once the product is ready to go to market, it requires multiple processes to get to the customer. Seasonality plays a key role in the annual oyster enterprise cycle:

- January to March- After the end of year holiday rush the first week of January is a time of rest and recuperation for the team. This period is followed by activities designed to create space in the fields for the oysters. After 18 months from catch, the oysters come to the farm and are graded and transferred from the initial sacks and placed in new sacks. They are then installed in new fields with careful attention given to protect the baby oysters from the ocean for the next few years.
- April to September – This period is characterized by tending the fields - shaking and rotating the sacks to provide maximum light and unclog the natural growing seaweed. The enterprise also spends time servicing the local and tourist traffic that frequent the Madec summer restaurant and family seafood store.
- October to December- In these months the harvesting and picking of all of the fields occurs (grading of 40,000 oysters /per hour), bringing them to fields closer to Prat-AR-Coum. The peak demand for oysters comes to a head in December just in time for the French Christmas celebration, which traditionally features oysters as a prime dish at the table.

Millions of baby oysters have journeyed for three years, battling nature to come forward and take the next phase of their journey to market. The Madec oysters go from the field into purification tanks before being sorted and graded for either retail sale in the Madec store, or packing for wholesale distribution around the world. Before the oysters can begin their journey to market, the production processes chain must take place. Grading levels begin at 000 – very large, 00-large, 0-bigger, 1-big and 2-medium-3 small, 4-smallest.

This is the area of business expertise for Caroline Madec, Yvon's daughter and next generation oysterwoman, who heads customer relations. The customer journey begins with advanced sales and marketing contact with Michelin-starred chefs and various wholesale markets in key geographical regions around the world. Since Caroline spent her formative business career training in Paris, she is familiar with communications and customer relations. Building relationships comes naturally for her. She understands the unique mindset of Michelin starred chefs like Guy Savoy and Alain Ducasse, typically servicing key customer relationships with 10-12 chefs at a time. These chefs all want high quality and freshness in their oysters at all costs. Caroline is just as comfortable visiting a supermarket manager or director as she is staffing a booth at a massive European trade show gastronomy exhibition.

Her customer relationship management duties also include hosting key seafood distributors for site visits at the family oyster farm. Her work ethic and durability merge with her stamina, much like road warriors for major corporations. No doubt her work ethic is in her genes, passed along from her father and her forefathers long ago. Caroline flies out of Brittany on a Sunday and is up early Monday morning in Dubai selling oysters to the luxury consumer markets. Her single most important task is making them aware of her family's terroir by the sea, the beauty and seafood bounty of Prat-AR-Coum.

While the packaging and shipping process is handled onsite, the distribution chain is just as important to getting the oysters in the hands of the consumer fresh and on time. This requires understanding and troubleshooting the various touch points in the distribution supply chain. Caroline often finds herself scheduling six or seven meetings a day with new staff in key distribution hubs around the globe, making sure they know the Madec family quality standards and commitment to excellence.

Last, but not least, is the human resource management component of the business. Annie Madec runs the books and manages the financial implications of the family business with the precision of a corporate accountant, coupled with the touch of a family matriarch. Meanwhile, Caroline handles the hiring and staffing of the field workers, packing team, seasonal restaurant workers, lift trucks, shipping connections, drudging boats and field workers.

Caroline Madec and Yvon Madec

Part 3. Madec Leadership Profiles

Leadership styles and traits-gender lens

The Madec generational legacy emphasizes multiple situational factors and particularly the nature of the work surrounding the complexity of the oyster business enterprise. Given the complexity of oyster farming, the contingency leadership theory emphasizes aligning the leader, follower and situational factors to achieve optimal results. Contingency leadership theory is useful in explaining and aligning the appropriate leadership style based on the leader, and is appropriately aligned with the Madec family management application.

Yvon is the current leader of the family enterprise with his daughter, Caroline, as the heir apparent generational Madec family member destined to be at the helm of the oyster enterprise. Yvon's leadership profile began with the foundational training and mentorship he received from his father Alain. Yvon describes his father as a man of few words. According to Yvon, he did not readily share the many intricacies of the oyster fields with him, rather, he expected Yvon to learn through doing. Yvon likely learned his high concern for the production process (oyster fields) and reliance on human capital processes to be sound and structured-task orientation through command and control leadership from his father. Given the close proximity of the oyster "handsman" to their product in the fields, Yvon needed to develop a high propensity for production, people and process. In leadership circles, this is recommended as the ideal leadership approach for a variety of situations. Yvon effortlessly takes charge to get the job done. Yvon directs not only Caroline, but other subordinates in the oyster fields, the packaging assembly plant and the retail aspects of the business.

Yvon Madec leadership traits

Yvon's autocratic-transactional approach to leadership strives to continually create the most economic and productive division of work by devising step-by-step procedures for each task involved in the oyster enterprise. He focuses intently on the division of work, and the tasks of field workers, to devise and implement the most efficient and cost-effective path to completing their work. Yvon mostly works on contingent plans in alignment with the unpredictable responses from nature and tidal activity.

For Yvon, leadership is simple enough: (1) select, train, teach and develop employees, (2) ensure that employees complete their work with a defined standard of consistency and quality, (3) ensure the proper division of labor and above all else, (4) keep their nose in the fields with the oysters. In this division of work, everyone has a key role, the leader (Yvon) strives to continually create the most economic and productive division of work by devising a step-by-step procedure for each task. Usually, autocratic-transactional leaders like to make all the decisions. In some cases, they may or may not consult with other associates or subordinates in the organization. This type of leader is confident, determined, and focused. They provide direction and expect those orders to be carried out successfully with little debate from others. This style of leadership is oftentimes highly effective and successful in production orientated enterprises. It leaves little room for debate and discussions and is accompanied by strict guidelines and standards of expected performance, often yielding consistent quality products.[5]

Yvon Madec-Day in the life profile
4:00 am – Yvon gets up
5:00 am – Arrival at the viviers to open the doors, turn on the machines & unfill the tanks
5:30 am –Prepare the schedule of the day, prepare the orders
6:30 am – Time to discover the today news
7: 00 – Arrival of the team
10:00- Departure for a tide to run on the fields
12:00 pm – Lunch time / small rest
1:30pm –Auction for crabs & scallops
3:00 pm – Grading
4:00 pm - Visit to his green house
5:00 pm – Last hour at the shop
7:30 pm Dinner
9:00 pm End of the day!

---

[5] http://www.managementskillsadvisor.com/authoritarian-leadership.html

Ultimately, the uniqueness of Yvon's leadership style is his ability to develop talent through adaptability, while maintaining a consistently high standard of product quality. He is goal-orientated, setting clear expectations so subordinates know what to do each day, by oyster field, by season and by tidal cycle. Yvon consistently makes sure his employees do their work according to established operating standards to make sure the work is being done correctly in the fields, the packaging area and customer relationship management processes. He is highly detail orientated. He watches every aspect of the oyster growing process with precision and instruction.

Exhibit 3. Yvon- Key leadership characteristics

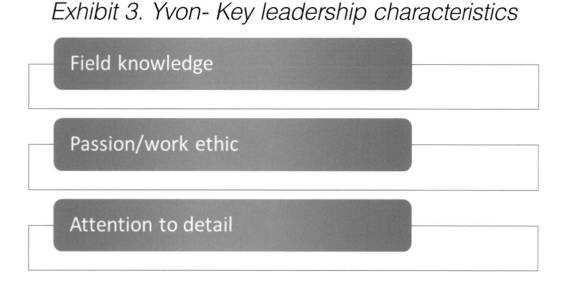

Field knowledge

Passion/work ethic

Attention to detail

Caroline Madec leadership traits

Caroline Madec's transformational leadership profile is grounded in her charismatic sensitivity towards her employees, often focusing on developing relationships with her employees based on trust, support and respect. This leadership approach bases the leader-follower relationship on unselfish service from leader to follower. In this style of employee centered leadership, leaders embrace the notion that those in the organization need empowerment, and in doing so, can achieve new heights of performance and creativity if given maximum support and individualized development.[6]

Caroline spends considerable time talking to her employees to get to know them during work to better understand their composition. She often works hard to build trust between herself and various employees of the family firm. Attitudes employees have about their jobs resonate in the attitude they exhibit during their interactions with leaders, co-workers, and customers. Caroline understands employees who enjoy their work and have a positive attitude will reflect this in their genuine desire to provide the best quality product and customer service possible.

First and foremost, Caroline focuses on creating positive work environments with high moral and job satisfaction. Perhaps the reason Caroline radiates transformational leadership skills is her own self-actualization. As a leader, Caroline is philosophical in her approach, yet exhibits high emotional intelligence capabilities. She is a conceptual thinker and is unafraid to view the family enterprise through a long-term lens. Caroline is keenly aware of the importance of work-life balance. She works extremely hard, yet knows the importance of being attentive to her young family. Caroline places high value on the human factor, listening carefully to her team members, sensitive to their growth and evolution within the family enterprise.

Much like her father, she was nurtured in a family enterprise system of discipline, hard work, and process improvement; however, she also prides herself on being non-conforming. She uses modern leadership traits and emotional intelligence to encapsulate a leadership approach focused on personal attention, charisma, passion and genuineness toward others. Her emotional intelligence reflects her ability to understand her emotions and those of others around her. Without this touch, a person can have the best training in the world, an incisive analytic mind, and an endless supply of smart ideas, but still won't make a great leader. Specifically, the relationship between emotional intelligence and the effectiveness of transformational leadership has been closely linked.[7] Softening the rigidity of the oyster enterprise production system, Caroline's transformational leadership approach is a unique balance of tradition and modern innovation in leadership style. She has a leadership style that transforms others and brings the best out of them without compromising her traditional values and father's transactional based process requirements.

---

[6] Greenleaf, Robert, K. (2003). *The Servant Leader Within: A transformative path.* (pp.45). New York/New Jersey. Paulist Press.

[7] Alimo-Mecalfe, B. (2002). Leadership and gender: A masculine past; a feminine future. Thematic paper for CERFE Project. Available at <http://www.womenand equalityunit.gov.uk/research/gender research_forum/ grf_papers_feb_june/cer_fin_gen_lea_pap.pdf>.

Day in the Life, a Profile of Caroline Madec
5:30 am – Breakfast reading e-mails from foreign customers
6:20 am – Drive my elder son to bus station
7:00 am - First call with Asian customers, beginning at
the company preparing of the first orders
7:30 am – Drive son Joseph to school, drop of mail at post and money at bank
8:00am – Packing oysters with the team or delivery to Brest
10:00 am - Visit fields at low tide
12:00 pm – Lunch and small rest
1:00 pm – Call with customers or journalist
2:30 pm - Meeting with supplier
4:30 pm – Picking up children at school
5:00pm – Book flights for a business trip, organizing booth decoration
8:00pm - End of the day calls with French friends and chefs

As a transformational leader, Caroline places a high emphasis on relationships with others.[8] In this area, she exhibits strength in relational components. Her high emotional intelligence capacity allows her to connect with others easily. She can empathize with others, she can coach them along and she can hold them accountable. She is not afraid to listen to their feedback, and she appreciates the pressure of work/life balance among her colleagues without compromising her family's commitment to quality of product.

As a charismatic leader, Caroline is both visionary and future orientated. She possesses superb communication skills and is eloquent, imaginative, and expressive to a wide audience of stakeholder groups (chefs, supermarket CEO's, foreign import/exporters, consumers, restaurant patrons and employees). Her self-confidence and moral conviction contribute to her unshakable confidence. She is willing to incur some level of personal risk in the name of preparing to carry on the family legacy while raising two young boys on her own. She generates relational power based on creating similar beliefs in others based on the family's devotion to quality and excellence often minimizing internal conflict by persistently staying the course.

---

[8] http://leadership.au.af.mil/documents/homrig.htm

Exhibit 4. Caroline-key leadership characteristics

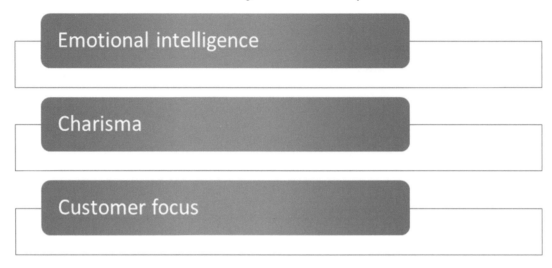

Gender leadership lens

As the gender landscape changes, women are embracing more leadership positions and trait characteristics. This is no different for the Madec family, with Caroline slated to take over the helm of the family enterprise.

Leadership styles are relatively consistent patterns of social interaction that typify leaders as individuals. For Caroline, even as more women enter into higher-level leadership positions, leaders, and subsequently "good" leaders, are still compared to and described in traditionally masculine terms. To break from this gendered framework, the concept of a gender-neutral leadership style may be more applicable. Using the concept of gender-neutral leadership style for the Madec family legacy would extend beyond the idea of "the great man conqueror" masculinity leadership style. The general-neutral idea is based on the premise that leadership styles are accessible by men and women equally and should be assessed accordingly. More neutral assessment of leadership capabilities can be extended to those in positions of influence who regularly:

- Challenge processes
- Inspire a shared vision
- Enable others to act

- Model the way forward
- Accomplish goals and objectives
- Encourage and incorporate others views
- Provide adequate return on investment
- Protect the environment

Despite the aforementioned evaluation of gender-neutral leadership, key gender-based barriers exist with respect to both men and women's evaluation of successful leadership. Side by side comparisons of gender-based disparities illustrate the need for women to be provided with more support mechanisms to achieve higher status in the organization.

The increase of women in the workforce is one of the most significant changes in the economy in the last 40 years. Women are increasingly taking over in industries throughout the world, and family businesses are not exempt from this trend. Succession planning, in terms of a time frame for the exit of an incumbent CEO and the entrance of an incoming CEO, is different when the next family business leader is female compared to an incoming male leader. Decisions about succession take place earlier if the next family business leader is female.[9] Having a female CEO could have an effect on business practices.

---

[9] David P. Evans / Procedia - Social and Behavioral Sciences 148 (2014) 543 – 550.

Exhibit 5. Gender Leadership Characteristics

	Female	Male
1. Lack of mentoring opportunities	70%	38%
2. Commitment to family	69%	53%
3. Exclusion from informal networks of communication	67%	25%
4. Lack of women role models	65%	35%
5. Failure of senior leadership to assume accountability for women's advancement	62%	22%
6. Stereotyping and preconceptions of women's roles and abilities	61%	27%
7. Lack of opportunities to take on visible and/or challenging assignments	54%	12%

Exhibit 5 highlights the gender gap in a few key areas, namely mentorship opportunities and stereotyping women's roles. The intersection of work/life balance and stereotyping women's roles in leadership reflect the largest disparity between men and women in leadership roles. For Yvon and Caroline, the gender identify role is more complex given the family component. Different generations, genders and rapidly evolving business environmental changes to the family business model provide regular unpredictability. Fortunately for Caroline, her father Yvon bucks the aforementioned trends in gender disparity among women leaders given their close father-daughter relationship and the prominent influence of Caroline's mother, Annie Madec, in the family enterprise hierarchy.

First and foremost, Caroline receives daily mentorship and commitment from both her mother Annie and her father Yvon, often learning the intricacies and historical knowledge transmission of the family oyster business on a daily basis. This is a unique blend of dual gender mentorship and support for Caroline. Caroline's mother provides both personal and professional advice to her daughter. Since Annie is so critical to the financial success of the family enterprise, she is able to impart her knowledge transmission to Caroline in that regard as well.

While commitment to family perceptions disparities between male and female genders is narrower than other categories, this is an area were Caroline struggles the most. Raising two young boys on her own while simultaneously learning the entire family enterprise is a challenge, as she has primary responsibility for sales and marketing, customer relationships, summer restaurant business and employee relationships. Learning the idiosyncrasies of the oyster fields proves especially difficult for Caroline with only so many hours in a day. Both her and her father realize the importance of Caroline visiting the fields with her father to extract key knowledge transmission that can only come from immersion in the fields.

This is easier said than done. With only so many hours in a day, Caroline is torn in many directions: raising her children, marketing, customer services, restaurant operations, packaging, shipping, distribution and new account management to name a few. Yvon is patient, and realizes Caroline is committed long-term to taking over the family business. As her young boys mature and grow into the family business one day themselves, Yvon knows time will favor his daughters needs for knowledge transmission at more intense levels across the many faces of the family enterprise.

While failure of senior leadership to assume accountability for women's advancement reflects a higher gap among women and men's perceptions, once again, Yvon and Annie buck this trend with respect to their daughter Caroline. Both Annie and Yvon recognize the importance of their daughters and grandsons sense of accomplishment. They encourage their children and grandchildren to find their own path. If it takes them out of the business, then so be it. They want their children to be naturally drawn to the family enterprise and love what they do. However, there are no free passes. If they are in the family business, they are in 100%. There are no shortcuts, the fragility of the oyster lifecycle does not allow for many mistakes or days off. Yvon goes to bed at night thinking about his oysters and is up at dawn tending to their every need.

Thomas A. Maier, PhD

Generational legacy- father and daughter

In today's rapidly growing global society, the convergence of cultures, diverse peoples, and their unique perspectives is at a heightened level thanks to technology, globalism and the proliferation of social media. These attributes of society will have a lasting impact on the next generation of Madec oyster farmers. Social scientists, who study the effects of population on society, use the term "generation" to refer to people born in the same general time span who share key life experiences, perceptions about the world and are primarily influenced by the era during which they are born and raised. The effects of those key life experiences tend to be relatively stable during the course of their lives.

More importantly, generational changes affect the way family business leaders manage their firms, and make traditional methods of succession and governance more complicated than ever. Each generational cohort comes with its own approach to life and work, profoundly redefining the status quo of families and their businesses. Identifying and understanding how such changes impact family businesses in the modern era offer unique insights for the Madec family legacy. Most importantly, researchers have found, older and younger workers have differing views on workplace expectations. Older workers expect long-term employment, promotions and status, while younger workers are more apt to enjoy technology and group collaboration with flexibility in their work. Employees with a lesser degree of comfort with technology (Baby Boomers) may find work less satisfying[10]. In today's work environment, this could lead to less engagement and motivation from older generations rather than younger ones.

For the Madec family legacy, job satisfaction and employee motivation are interrelated factors in their multigenerational workplace. Caroline especially recognizes that work itself and job responsibility lead to the greatest number of satisfied employees. Given the complex nature of the world's multi-generational workforce, the Madecs understand the importance of adaptive leadership.

Adaptive leadership capacity refers to working well with others across diverse perspectives and focusing on the importance of employee satisfaction. Adaptive leaders like Yvon and Caroline engage others through shared meaning in order to find opportunities to recognize their employee's accomplishment rather than faults. Caroline has clear values and the adaptive

---

[10] Zemke, R., Raines, C., Filipczak, B. (2000). Generations at Work. New York: American Management Association.

ability to discern when it is best to lead or to follow. Both Yvon and Caroline understand human interaction is often the key differentiator in virtually all aspects of their family oyster farming enterprise. This human centered approach to leadership supports their belief that workplace organizational processes are fluid, open and flexible. This environment mirrors the issues related to natures unpredictability, market turbulence and other disruptive elements of their global oyster enterprise.

For both Yvon and Caroline, their distinct key life experiences and generational knowledge acquisition has developed a leadership persona that determines their feelings toward authority, the future of the family enterprise and the customers they serve.[11] Like generations of oyster farmers before them, Yvon and Caroline are faced with situations involving employees who are unable to work together productively, often due to differing perspectives in ages, values, morals, and interaction style. The effects of these multigenerational differences in gastronomy have arrived at the Madec doorstep. Workers are no longer remaining in the workforce for long careers, leading to turnover. Higher turnover is creating environments where employees often experience confusion, frustration, and stress when working with individuals outside their own generational groups or cultural similarities.

In the fast-paced global economy, with increased pressure for higher productivity and quicker results, the demand for collaboration and compromise has intensified for the Madec family. Multigenerational differences in perspectives create fertile ground for conflict and an "us vs. them" mentality that results in job dissatisfaction, high employee turnover, and decreased productivity. Within the gastronomy world in particular, generational orientation is also likely to determine what individuals want from work, what kind of workplace environment they desire, and how they plan to satisfy those wants and desires (work/life balance). Employees from different generations may have problems understanding others' perspectives about work and work ethic, creating stress, confusion, and frustration in a demanding workplace like the oyster farming enterprise.[12]

The primary generational groups may hold different views about the world, country, work, and self-development than Yvon and Caroline. The forces of change and adaptability vary across roles, and the understanding and application of this "fit" has been shown to produce more

---

[11] Gursoy, D., Maier, T., Chi, C. (2008). "Generational differences: an examination of work values and generational gaps in the hospitality workforce," *International Journal of Hospitality Management*, 27 (3), 448–458.

[12] Zemke, R., Raines, C., Filipczak, B. (2000). *Generations at Work*. New York: American Management Association.

efficient and effective companies in terms of their visions, missions, goals, and objectives. Positive inquiry can be used as a means of facilitating dialogue and bridging the gap created by divergent generational interests, thereby promoting a positive environment and commitment of employees to work collaboratively to achieve the vision and goals of the organization. Understanding those perspectives can help smooth work flow processes, reduce turnover and create a vibrant work culture. The following is a brief profile of each generational group presented:[13]

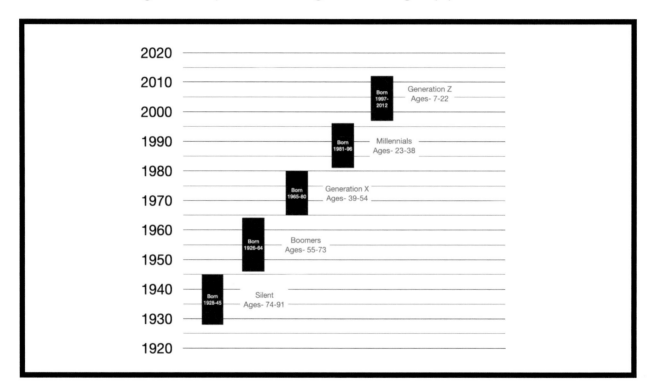

Yvon Madec - Baby Boomer (1946-1964)

Yvon, like many Frenchmen, has views steeped in French gastronomic heritage, influenced by his father at a very early age. Yvon recounts "it started in the fields. My father was a man of few words. He demonstrated exceptional leadership to me through his actions and work ethic."

---

[13] Cook, Ross, Inc. (2004). *Managing a Multigenerational Workforce: The diversity manager's toolkit.* Silver Springs, MD: Author.

It is remarkable to see how Yvon took those early influences from his father. As a baby boomer, he believes results are achieved through hard work and perseverance. Yvon was raised in an era of optimism, environmental disasters and financial exigency. He grew up in a two-parent household with the mother as primary caregiver and the father as sole income earner. Key characteristics of his baby boomer generation include face-to-face communication and hard work.

This generation is motivated by receiving symbols of recognition, titles, monetary rewards, special job perks, peer recognition and symbols of status. Boomers, for the most part, grew up in two-parent households, attended safe schools, lived during a period job security and post-war prosperity. Many, reflecting back on their lives, realize they have focused the majority of their time on their jobs and want to find a greater balance between work and leisure. Boomers like Yvon often feel younger workers need to carry the load and put in their time before advancing and accumulating equity in the enterprise.

Caroline Madec - GENX (1965–1980)

Caroline has the leadership characteristics of a GenX leader. Her leadership values and actions are consistent with team building, high employee engagement, and the importance of partnerships. She recognizes that with diversity, comes new perspectives, ideas, and insights. She is experimental and entrepreneurial - learning through both traditional and experiential means. She is more secure with insecurity and change, committed to making a life, not just a living. Caroline successfully leads across a wide continuum of leadership styles. However, that same spectrum of leadership offers complexity of role identity for Caroline, often shifting between leader (boss), follower (subordinate), daughter and situation (time of year and state of the oyster cycle).

For Caroline, remembering what she observed in her youth, Gen-Xers generally are leery of devoting long hours to their jobs that keep them away from their family and activities outside of work. Different from Boomers, Gen-Xers desire to have a better work-life balance and view their jobs as a means to an end, rather than as a way of defining who they are as a person based on their career path. This mindset among Gen-Xers often leads to tension and conflict with workers from the Baby Boomer generation. Unlike their older coworkers, Gen-Xers are not willing to sacrifice their lifestyle, health, and friends to jump at promotional opportunities. Obviously, this is different for Caroline as she is working hard to take on the next generation of the Madec oyster family legacy.

As members of the generation following the Baby Boomers, Gen-Xers were born into a rapidly changing social climate dominated by social and civil unrest, and advances in science and technology, that moved the average citizen into the computer age. On the job, they tend to be skeptical of the system, fiercely independent, in control, and view job freedom as a reward. They seek training opportunities that enhance their skills and want fast feedback. Unimpressed by titles and status, they work to live rather than live to work, preferring an environment that is informal and fun.

Millennials (1981-1996)

As the second youngest generational group, Millennials have grown up in a fast-paced, technology-dominated society. As employees, Millennials thrive on direction, structure, and stimulation in the workplace. They have had a stable upbringing and were involved in more social activities and sports compared to Gen-Xers. For the Madec family, their primary workforce composition of Millennials tends to be social, have a sense of civic engagement and want to know that their work makes a difference in the world. Although Millennials, they are fast learners, impatient, and when they question authority, it is usually for the right reasons. Millennials want their supervisors and other co-workers to provide directions with clear descriptions of the task or project to be completed. Brainstorming often is difficult for Millennials and they respond better to specific benchmarks as guides. Millennials like structure to their jobs, especially in terms of having tasks broken into smaller sub-tasks and having the work to be completed modeled by their co-worker or supervisor. Finally, Millennials have highly active lives and are skilled at multi-tasking. They prefer work that is stimulating and allows them the freedom to develop their own way of self-organizing their work.

GenZ (1997-2012)

Technology is a driving force in the way people communicate and interact with one another across and within generations. For instance, Baby Boomers had the expansion of television influencing their lifestyles and ushering the consumer age, changing their lifestyles and connection to the world. On the other hand, the GenX generation cohort grew up when the computer revolution began. Millennials came of age during the internet explosion. The internet explosion led to the digital progression that is most unique facet of GenZ.

The advancement of digital technology ushered in the the smart phone device that has become the primary means of socialization and communication among younger generations. The onset of social media has disrupted the way people connect and consume information and entertainment. For GenZ cohort members born after 1996, the technology integration has been natural. This reliance on technology has caused significant changes in youth attitudes and lifestyles.

While Generation Z's views are similar with Millennials in many areas, they are distinct in their views regarding the role of social media in their lives. Gen-Zers are less inclined to get their news from social media channels, and are more apt to receive it from their own generational social circles rather than traditional media channels. Therefore, social influencers impact the view of younger generations more so than any other generational cohort. Gen-Zers' views about climate change are virtually identical to those of Millennials and not much different from those of Gen-Xers. About half in all three generational cohorts say the earth is getting warmer due to human activity. Boomers are somewhat more skeptical of this than Gen-Zers or Millennials. Members of the Silent Generation are least likely to say this (38%) and are more likely to say the earth is warming mainly due to natural patterns (28%) than Gen-Zers, Millennials and Gen-Xers.[14]

When managing a multi-generational workforce and conducting business across the globe, both Yvon and Caroline appreciate multiple perspectives of work and leadership. They bring into conversation policy and strategy discussions of a more holistic view of the family workplace. It is important for them to carefully examine organizational processes and understand their own generational effects from life style, life values, personality, and perspectives of work within the family context.

This leadership awareness of generational complexity, has been shown to produce more efficient and effective results for the family enterprise in terms of overall vision, business diversification, risk aversion and enterprise sustainability. Both Yvon and Caroline often facilitate improved performance and retention of employees. Establishing cooperative interaction between different generational group members requires organizational leaders who are

---

[14] Pew Reserch report. https://www.pewsocialtrends.org/2019/01/17/generation-z-looks-a-lot-like-millennials-on-key-social-and-political-issues/

providing events that enable employees to interact with each other. Caroline especially knows that generational integration in the workplace benefits both the company and employees. When the organization is perceived as a fun place to work, the productivity is more likely to increase moral and job satisfaction. This leads to higher employee retention levels, and the generation of a solid reputation as a good place to work — which better enables the enterprise to attract high quality employees.

Father and daughter relationship

More importantly, any father-daughter relationship may be difficult in the context of family legacy and oyster farming. Caroline has grown up around her father in the oyster business which has been characterized by male centric work, long hours, unpredictability, strategic thinking and unending commitment to excellence. As a result, Caroline is very confident, capable, and determined. She wants to please her father by achieving success on her own. She has done this through her efforts in leaving the family business early in her career to go to Paris to perfect her marketing and customer relationship management skills, while also experiencing and absorbing urban living.

Caroline is not necessarily an "oysterman" like her father. Yvon has the field mentality grounded in him by his father. Conversely, Caroline is a charismatic businesswoman with an entrepreneurial spirit. Caroline is smart, sensitive, and creative. She is a talented leader with a wide range of skills and abilities: (1) sophistication, (2) focus, (3) charisma (4) passion for oyster farming like her father and (5) drive for success. She is also a daughter who respects and loves her father, mother, sister and works hard to prove her capabilities. Caroline exhibits a self-pride and commitment to being the best. Given the duality of being a daughter and business partner, she is conflicted, genuinely not wanting to disappoint her father and boss. Her inner drive and enterprise stamina are shared with her father, and evident in her dedication and work ethic.

Work/Life balance

For Yvon, the work life balance equation is simple. Work is life. For a man who lives and dies by the fate of the oyster, he is at home on the water, in and around his beloved oysters. For Yvon, a good day is a day spent tending to the fields, thinking ahead and making key strategic decisions about his precious oyster stock scattered around Brittany. An ongoing, strategic chess match with nature. By his side is his wife of 50 years, Annie Madec. Annie and Yvon have made a dynamic team duo. He runs the business, and she runs the financial aspects of the bustling global family enterprise. For those in a family enterprise, much like the Prat-AR-Coum tides, the ebbs and flows of the enterprise are grounded in a common daily bond among husband and wife.

On the other hand, the heir apparent leader Caroline, spends her days immersed in all aspects of the business enterprise while raising her boys and tending to the needs of her family. A dual role with the added pressure of being a single mother. Her daily routine on the job is intertwined between the alignment of field production, packaging and distribution. She merges the interests of Michelin chefs and worldwide customer demands with field level productivity outputs, not to mention the summer customer-facing Madec café on the esteemed banks of Prat-AR-Coum alongside the picturesque Aber-Benoît.

Knowledge transmission

Successful generational family leadership is linked positively to optimal mentoring success. The transformational Madec leadership approach is consistent with requirements of effective mentoring because it builds follower (protégé) trust. By exhibiting idealized influence, transformational leaders (Yvon) are viewed by their followers (Caroline) as a trustworthy symbol of success and accomplishment. A type of visualized role modeling and personal projection. In leadership theory, a critical component of any successful leader is their ability to execute succession planning through the development of others around them.

Succession planning can be favorably influenced through the mentorship process. In family enterprise circles, there is a close link between effective leadership style and mentorship success rates. A key component of any family business leader is their ability to mentor. Strong mentorship success is not only in the physical and visible realms. Intellectual stimulation is said to be a strong contributor to protégé development. Yvon is not only technically sound, but he is able to provide intellectual stimulation to his daughter Caroline because of his lived experience and originality in the fields. His craftsmanship and leadership style has been absorbed and painstakingly passed down from Madec generation to generation.

His words have stronger meaning, derived from a proven track record bolstered through years of trial and tribulation. His focus on success and inspirational meaning creates the possibility of success for others beyond what they can see in themselves, especially his daughter Caroline. This focus on "other" is a classical transformational leadership characteristic. For Caroline, this can be a challenge as much as an opportunity. Her father has a high bar for success and that can come with its own set of difficulties. Caroline understands the gift she has received from her father, that she possesses within herself too. Freely spirited, Yvon provides inspirational vision of the future for his daughter and grandsons based on a trustful, responsible relationship that warrants security in those who desire to sustain the Madec legacy into the future.

Part 4. Madec Sustainability Practices

Environmental stewardship

Throughout the planet, aquaculture encapsulates a broad and significant economic stimulus in and around rural coastal areas that are often otherwise economically depressed. The aquamarine based activities that occur in and around the coastal watershed provides an ideal occupational opportunity for *ostreiculture* like the Madec family. The waterways and their sustainable development have preserved the character and ambience of Brittany communities like Prat -AR-Coum and generational residents like the Madec family since 1898. They have utilized and transmitted their local knowledge and skills from generation to generation, allowing themselves to remain economically and culturally tied to the tranquil Prat-AR-Coum marine environment in which they live. The various infrastructures of racks, cages, nets, ropes, trays, boats and purification tanks.

That tranquil and pristine coastal environment was abruptly disturbed on March 16, 1978, when the supertanker Amoco Cadiz, owned by Amoco International Oil Company was shipping 220,000 metric tons of crude oil from Iran and Saudi Arabia to Rotterdam. Unfortunately, as the super-sized oil tanker approached the shores of Western Europe, it sailed into a severe storm and its steering gear failed off the Brittany coast.

The Amoco Cadiz captain radioed for help to no avail. The vessel, with its 220,000 metric tons of crude oil aboard, grounded, spilling more than 35% of the crude into the ocean, damaging over 200 miles of coastline in Northern Brittany. The environmental devastation had an enormous impact on the people of Brittany and the biological ecosystem and marine-based industries including tourism, fisheries and oyster production. Sea walls, beach coastlines, piers and personal property were all severely damaged. Bretons were without work and many Brittany industries witnessed an unsurmountable reduction in their sales due to the fear of oil contamination. Even the sale of uncontaminated oysters and fish was affected by the suspicion that they had been harvested in Brittany. The tourism trade in non-polluted areas in Brittany and in the neighboring regions slowed down dramatically. At the time oysters, (*crassostrea gigas*), collected from the oiled estuaries showed high levels of *Amoco Cadiz* oil fractions indicated that the region had been chronically-exposed to petroleum hydrocarbons of *Amoco Cadiz* origin.

At the time, Breton production was expected around 7000 metric tons, representing 7% of the French national oyster market. All the oyster beds had been heavily contaminated and suffered the most damage. Many oysters were killed, and many others were tainted and simply could not be re-sold. There were exceptional costs in the attempted moving of oysters to clean water, as well as the physical damage to the oyster beds and the sediments. Oysters could not be returned to the parks in time to permit proper development before marketing, so more than 8000 metric tons were destroyed. Given the three-year growth to market timeline, the oyster beds in the affected areas could not be sown with new stocks while the oil contamination remained, five years were needed before the normal production level could be reached.

According to Yvon, besides the family's stock being lost, Brittany oysters were affected by bad publicity. This favored a dramatic increase in oyster production in new areas, fueling market expansion and strong competitors to Brittany. The major costs of clean-up of the oyster beds and business losses amounted to 67.95 million francs during the period 1978-1983. The Madec's rebounded and persevered through the crisis. While it nearly devastated their family enterprise, they recognized the need and importance to be stewards of the environment in order to maintain clean growing waters and ensure their own future viability. They also understand that shellfish culture also promotes and enhances biodiversity by creating structure and habitat for other marine species. Shellfish beds provide a larger variety and biomass of associated invertebrates and finfish than a similar area without shellfish. The oyster culture technique is rather simple. The young oysters are deposited on the sea bottom and grow until their size is appropriate for harvesting. Oysters must be harvested and marketed at exactly the proper time; if they are allowed to mature too fully, the flesh will lose its tenderness and flavor and the oysters will have no value in the market.

Export trade and a global market

Globalization has brought with it the need for more intensive labor management competencies in service businesses given the heightened multicultural and multigenerational awareness. This is all coming together within the organizational context and new generational work culture. Increasingly, the Madec's macro-perspective of leadership and French culture considers the entire societal meaning, and the role that society plays in their generational enterprise.

Conversely, the micro-perspective entails more the individual employees' performance in the organization as it pertains to the business at hand.

Many factors have helped shape and define the Madec's global oyster enterprise: the global economy, political forces, changing demographics, technological trends, pandemic outbreaks, seasonal business cycles, shipping distribution, tariffs and government regulations. The oyster business provides both a perishable product and requires constant service. It remains a "high touch" rather than "high tech enterprise." Not many global enterprises today are so labor intensive. For Yvon and Caroline that prediction will be put to the test in the next decade with the wave of technological advancements in shipping, distribution and customer acquisition in the digital age.

What is in store for the *ostreiculture* entrepreneur leader of the future? In many respects, Yvon has been leading ahead of the times, after all, he was present at the helm of the Madec family enterprise during its most turbulent times and has forged ahead diversifying and strategically positioning the family business against unpredictable risks. He has endured major economic downturns and has settled the family into a global enterprise spanning three continents, with no sign of slowing down. Most importantly, he has succeeded, with his daughter Caroline by his side, through adaptation within the rigorous and complex organizational context of the *ostreiculture* industry, an industry that relies heavily on adaption to stay ahead of mother nature's unpredictability.

As the future leader of the Madec family enterprise, the big question for Caroline is generating the advanced capability to recognize the importance of empowering others while also ensuring organizational sustainability. She says, "we have to produce more for less, and with greater speed than we've ever done before." Caroline knows the only way to do that is through the empowerment of people. Whether the competitive environments are international, regional, or local, the sustainability and competitive challenges facing their business makes it necessary to continually develop personnel. Like her father, she recognizes the need for a solid handsman in the field.

Family business and succession planning

For Yvon (patriarch) and Annie (matriarch) Madec, implementing a succession plan requires them to select the right governance structure for their family business for its long-term sustainability. Most successful succession plans occur when family governance processes and structures support frequent and transparent communication among family members, helping them define who they are as a group and what they want to achieve as a family.

Whether formal or informal succession planning, the level of family governance development is linked to how strong family members identify with the enterprise as a whole. Family businesses can implement different governance tools, ranging from a family constitution, formal family meetings, a family council, or even the use external consultants to manage and address family issues.

For both Yvon and Annie, planning for a smooth succession starts with recognizing that it will be one of the most complicated transitions that the family will experience. They recognize that it is never too early to start discussing succession, and that the costs of getting the succession planning wrong will be nothing short of catastrophic for the business. Yvon, in particular, knows these challenges mean that family members must focus strongly on the business at hand, giving it their undivided attention.

Yvon knows all too well, long before decisions will be made about specific succession to Caroline, the family must agree on the overarching issues. Whether family unity will take precedence over wealth creation, whether all members of the family will have an equal ownership right and voice in decisions, and whether decisions will be based purely on merit and the best interests of the business. These guiding principles will provide the framework for more specific decisions as to when the handover takes place.

What lies behind the reluctance of Yvon to openly discuss succession planning and tackle the challenges head-on? Succession planning sits at the intersection of family considerations, which typically involve emotions and feelings, and business considerations, which are typically driven by earned performance and economic viability. This duality of emotional and financial concerns can make succession an especially complex topic keeping Yvon and Annie up at night. No doubt it's difficult for Yvon to finally let go and to talk about relinquishing the helm. is personal identity is strongly linked to the family oyster enterprise and love of the water.

As the family patriarch and transactional leader with a strong personality, his formidable capabilities and long, distinguished record of managing all aspects of the business often casts a lengthy shadow over younger generations in line (Caroline). In such cases, succession can be a nearly taboo subject that is difficult to broach. Even when succession is high on the leadership agenda, like other family businesses, the Madec family enterprise faces significant challenges in getting it right.

Yvon and Annie know striking the right balance between the business's needs, and family members' aspirations, can be complex. Addressing this complexity often calls for creative approaches—beyond the traditional CEO-and-chairperson model. Yvon and Annie are less formal and have frequent conversations surrounding the family enterprise with siblings Caroline and her sister Virginie. Despite their lack of a formal succession plan, the likelihood that the Madec family business will stay in the hands of a family member in the future is very high.

Families may hesitate to plan succession because they are uncertain how the interests, choices and decisions of different family members will play out over years or decades. That's not the case for the Madec's. They have started planning knowing that along the way they may need to anticipate potential scenarios for how the family will evolve. For Yvon and Annie, issues to consider include the next generational legacy and whether both of their daughters, or just Caroline, are interested in the family business as a source of full or part-time employment or purely as an investment. Moreover, marriages or the sudden demise of a family member or potential successors can bring forward uncertainty. That is why it is important to plan a succession process and outcomes that will work for different foreseeable scenarios.

Most importantly, most successful family succession choice is based on the Carolines level of interest in the business. Since Caroline is integrated into the business now, her business interest and demonstrated work ethic is very high. Beyond interest levels in the position, qualifications, self-commitment and competence are the core criteria on which the family businesses will move forward. The need to decide whether to select a successor from within or outside the family is already underway. Since Caroline and her sister Virginie are the only internal family members, the decision is less difficult. At the present time, Virginie has expressed little desire to be the next in line at the helm. Caroline, on the other hand, is willing to take it on. Accordingly, both a formal (contractual plan) and informal plan (training knowledge transmission) have been put in place for how she will prepare for the leadership role and gain acceptance as the leader by other family members and company employees.

Eventually, Yvon must be willing to let Caroline emerge from under his shadow and take charge as planned. In some cases, families may hesitate to plan succession because they are uncertain how the interests, choices, and decisions of different family members will play out over years or decades. Although things may change along the way, both Yvon and Annie often anticipate the potential scenarios for how the family will evolve. Key scenarios include:[15]

---

[15] Boston Consulting Group. *Succeeding with Succession Planning in Family Businesses*
https://www.bcg.com/enus/publications/2015/leadership_talent_growth_succeeding_with_succession_planning_family_businesses

- Has Yvon committed to a fixed retirement date?
- Has Yvon and Annie evaluated the pipeline of leadership talent within its younger generation? Have they looked at potential leaders who come from within the business but not within the family?
- Has Yvon and Annie defined a succession model and determined the timing for selecting Caroline so that she has a sufficient opportunity to prepare for the leadership role and build credibility before her father retires?
- Does the family understand how it will accommodate the aspirations of other family members not selected for leadership roles, in order to maintain harmony and avoid discord during the transition to new leadership?

In many cases, family businesses will find that the answers to questions like these indicate the need to devote significantly more time and attention to succession planning. Most importantly, Yvon and Annie know they need to continue having open and candid discussions about succession related issues with Caroline to ensure the business will thrive for generations to come. These discussions are never easy, but they are essential. Getting succession wrong can be an irreversible and often fatal mistake for a family business. Key performance criteria include the following:[16]

1. *Setting expectations, philosophy, and values upfront.* Family businesses that thrive and succeed across generations are those that possess a core philosophy and set of values linked not to wealth creation, but to a sense of community and purpose. The Madecs have done an excellent job in this regard. This step is essential when it comes to succession planning and must be done up front, often and even if the specific mechanics of succession come later.

2. *Independently assess what's right for the business.* Although the best interests of the business and the family may seem indistinguishable to some family members, in reality, the optimal decisions from the business's perspective may differ from what family members want for themselves. For the Madecs, this distinction makes it essential to consider what is right for the business independent of family preferences when developing a

---

[16] Boston Consulting Group. Succeeding with Succession Planning in Family Businesses https://www.bcg.com/enus/publications/2015/leadership_talent_growth_succeeding_with_succession_planning_family_businesses

succession plan. It is therefore important to think about succession from a purely business perspective before making any adjustments based on family preferences. This allows Yvon to be transparent and deliberate with Caroline in the trade-offs they may have to make when managing any competing priorities.

3. *Develop the successor's capabilities broadly.* The challenges of leading a family business are even greater than those faced by leaders of other businesses. A family business should invest in developing the successor's capabilities and grooming them for leadership. The preparation should occur in phases starting at a young age—even before the successor turns 18. The Madec's have done this exceptionally well. It is evident this occurred between Yvon and his father, and in the next generation, between Yvon and his daughter Caroline. In addition to leadership and entrepreneurship, as successor Caroline needs to develop values aligned with the family's aspirations for the business and its role in the French society—capabilities that constitute stewardship of the company. Given the rapidly increasing complexity of global business in the twenty-first century, Caroline's experience outside the family business definitely broadened her perspective.

4. *External career development experience.* Some of the best-managed family businesses have robust career-development processes for family members that are the equal to world-class talent management and capability-building processes. Given the rapidly increasing complexity of business in the twenty-first century, Both Yvon and Annie recognized early on that it was important for Caroline to expand her horizons beyond the family business. Her stint in marketing and customer relations in Paris suited her well.

5. *Define a clear and objective selection process.* A company needs to define a selection process to implement its succession model—whether selecting a successor exclusively from the family, or considering nonfamily executives as well. For Yvon, the selection process is based on articulated expectations of his successor, clearly delineating roles among family governance bodies and addressing who will lead the process and make decisions.

   An early start is especially important if several family members are under consideration or the potential exists to divide the business to accommodate leadership aspirations. To obtain an objective perspective on which members of the younger generation have the greatest leadership potential, some families have benefited from the support of external advisors in evaluating talent and running the selection process.

6. *Build credibility through a phased transition.* It's important for successors to build their credibility and authority through well-defined phases of a transition into the leadership role. Caroline has started with a phase of shadowing her father to learn about his routines, priorities, and ways of operating in the fields. Next, she will gradually act more as a chief operating officer, managing the operations closely but still deferring to her father on strategic decisions. Ultimately, Caroline can take over as the CEO and chairperson and drive the family business forward when Yvon is ready to step away.

   It is important to emphasize that the family member who assumes leadership of the business does not necessarily also become the head of the family, with responsibility for vision setting, family governance and alignment, and wealth management. The transition of family leadership can be a distinct process. Each phase of the transition often takes between two and six months. The transition should be defined by clear milestones and commensurate decision rights. A sudden transition can be disruptive, which is especially harmful if the intent is to maintain continuity in the family business's direction and strategy.

7. *Ask departing leaders to leave but not disappear.* Most leaders bring something distinctive to a family business. In this case it's Yvon's inherent knowledge of the oyster fields and the ebb and flow of the tides. Holding onto this distinctiveness in a transition is essential, but requires a delicate balance. Although Yvon should eventually relinquish managerial responsibility for the business, he should remain connected to Caroline in one or two areas where he brings the truly distinctive value that made the family business successful under his guidance.

   However, it will be important for Yvon to be involved in these activities through a formal process, rather than at his own personal preference and discretion. Yvon must stay available to guide his daughter Caroline if she seeks this advice. To help Yvon strike this balance and overcome his reluctance to let go, he could create a "glide path" plan that sets out how he will turn over control in phases and transition into other activities while Caroline assumes control and builds credibility. Moreover, the family should also consider the need to adjust aspects of the company's governance model when Yvon hands over the reins. Although such adjustments can be made outside the context of succession, they often become particularly relevant after transitions to the second or third generation. A strong leader's hands-on governance approach is often no longer sustainable for the next generation, creating the need to divide and formalize roles and institutionalize many business processes.

Closing

The Madec family legacy offers a behind the scenes glimpse of a multi-generational French *ostreiculture* enterprise. Passed from generation to generation since 1898. This story examined their family-centered business model and succession planning through the lens of leadership philosophy in French gastronomy. In this multi-generational profile, Yvon's accomplishments and entrepreneurial spirit were uncovered through discovery of their family's unique regional terroir, ocean paradise and the aber products they yield. We looked deep into Yvon's craft as an oysterman, and the leadership composition of him and his daughter Caroline, divided by generations, yet unified by a common interest in refinement and perfection. The family succession is well underway to the next generation. As the future unfolds, Yvon will sail his last trip at the helm of the family enterprise soon, followed by the maiden voyage of Caroline Madec, leading the family into the next generation of *ostreiculture.*

About the Author

Thomas A. Maier has a PhD in leadership philosophy and a master's degree in human development/international relations. He has been successful in producing several refereed academic scholarly publications. His published academic journal articles have appeared in hospitality's top-refereed journals. The focus of Dr. Maier's research falls into two distinct categories: multigenerational leadership and revenue optimization. His ethnographic series of family-generational biographies feature Frances finest gastronomic families in food, wine and oyster farming. Parisian Michelin Chef *** Guy Savoy, Hospitality Leadership Lessons in French Gastronomy, Bordeaux Winemaker -Jean Pierre Amoreau, Generational Leadership and Sustainable Practices in French Winemaking and Brittany Oyster Farmer Yvon Madec, The Madec Family Legacy: Lessons In Leadership.